The five walks in this book have been selected to give you a real ... ...cinating, and often overlooked, corner of Cor... ... varied and attractive countryside ... ...tes, and nearly all start or pass through vill... ...ments.

Before you set out

Times and distances given for the walks are approximate, and allow for detours and rests. Some routes include short cuts (marked on the maps with brown dotted lines). The routes follow well-worn paths, bridleways and lanes, and most of them are designated public rights of way. Stout footwear is advisable, as many walks include farmland stretches which can be very muddy after rain and in winter.

Follow the Countryside Code
Keep to the footpaths and leave gates as you find them. Some walks pass through fields which may contain livestock. Always keep your dog under control, do not disturb wildlife unnecessarily or uproot wild plants. Leave no litter.

Public rights of way

Most of the routes follow public rights of way and it is advised that the **1:25,000 Ordnance Survey Explorer 103 Map is used** in conjunction with this book. Some permissive paths have also been used tand these may not be shown on the Explorer map. **Permissive paths are open by courtesy of the current landowner and are not designated rights of way.**

Walk 3

Maen Quarry

Walk 1

Brill Hill

Bosahan Woods

Brill

Walk 2

Walk 4

High Cross

Walk 5

Constantine

Ponjeravah

Polwheveral

Trenarth Bridge

Naphene Downs

Tolvan Cross

Scott's Quay

Port Navas

Gweek

Helford Passage

Helford River

Helford

Constantine churchtown in 1908. ▶
Churchtown was the setting for a violent struggle, one night in November 1828, between two customs officers and a large band of smugglers, armed with pistols, bludgeons and knives. The officers attempted to seize several horses laden with spirits, whereupon the smugglers retaliated, 'feloniously assaulting the officers... so that the life of one of them is despaired of'. A reward of £300 was offered for information leading to an arrest.

St Constantine

Little is known about the man who gave his name to the church *(pictured, above in the Lady Chapel window)*, except that he was one of the few Celtic saints to be a Cornishman. He is thought to have been a violent 5th century chieftain or king – possibly of the west country kingdom of Dumnomia – who put aside his sword and became a monk. His Feast Day is March 9th, still celebrated in the village today *(see below)*.

If you stand on Brill Hill, looking down on Constantine's huddle of houses, you might think that invasions, wars and social upheaval had all bypassed this rural community. Well, think again...

Invading Romans were the first to set camp here, their galleys loading up with locally-streamed tin. Raids by Saxons and Vikings followed, until the Normans arrived, carving up the church-lands into feudal manors. In the 16th century, it was Constantine yeomen who began a rebellion that was to set the west aflame. Three centuries later, Constantine's tin and copper mines helped fuel the industrial revolution, and Victorian Britain's cities and ports were built from Constantine granite. Both World Wars took their toll on the village, refugees and evacuees arrived in 1940, and the Helford River creeks were a launch pad for D-Day invasion forces.

To the manor born

The village began as a few huts gathered around the monastery of St Constantine, its lands stretching from the granite outcrops of Carvedras down to Polwheveral Creek. Following the Norman Conquest, the land was divided into feudal estates, with almost everyone working for the lords of the manors. This agricultural community grew slowly – in 1377 the parish numbered only 390, and it took another 300 years to double. By the 1500s, everyone in the parish would have spoken Cornish – including the many Bretons who'd arrived seeking work as labourers and servants. It's hardly surprising that this Celtic community would violently resist the imposition of the English prayerbook *(see panel opposite)*.

Constantine Feast in 1913. ▶
Still going strong today, the Feast used to be a drunken riotous affair, in which a 'mock mayor' (paid 7/6) was dragged in a cart around the village, delivering speeches and lambasting those responsible for any scandals. The procession would start at the Queen's Arms and end at Polwheveral where the mayor was tipped into the river. In 1857 the new vicar, Revd Rickards, was so disgusted by the orgy that he prevented its recurrence.

A snapshot of the village in the 1900s

It wasn't until the 1830s that Constantine became the village we know today, its Fore Street cottages built to house an expanding population of tin, copper and granite workers. By the 1900s this industrial boom was over, and many miners and quarrymen had emigrated, but if you were walking down Fore Street in 1914, you'd still have seen a bustling village scene, with half-a-dozen shops, a post office, two pubs, a smithy and two carpentry workshops all doing brisk business. The village had two schools, three cobblers, a tailor, a draper and a doctor, and regular horse-buses to Falmouth, Helston and Redruth. The Methodist Chapel, enlarged in 1879, was enjoying congregations of 400 or more, and the parish church had just extended its overcrowded churchyard.

Constantine today

The cobblers and blacksmiths have gone but, a century later, the village is still thriving. Remarkably, in this supermarket age, it has a grocery, a butcher, an electrical shop, craft gallery, taxi service, post office and off-licence. The Queen's Arms is going strong, and there's a licensed social club. There's an outstanding primary school, several builders, carpenters, and home-based businesses ranging from baby clothes to website design. The hub of village activity is the Tolmen Centre – an arts centre, cafe and museum – and there are a bewildering number of societies, clubs and sports teams. Constantine is currently home to five Cornish bards, and since 1991 has been twinned with Pont-Croix in Brittany, an appropriate relationship, given that many villagers are probably descended from Bretons who lived here in the Middle Ages.

Constantine rebels

When Edward VI's commissioner, William Body, arrived in Helston on 5 April 1548, to strip the church of Catholic relics, the local fisherman and farmers decided enough was enough. Led by the Kylter brothers, yeomen of Constantine, and Martin Geffrey, priest of St Keverne, a 1000-strong crowd marched on the town, and found Body removing the precious church jewels and icons. He fled to a house in Church Street, but the throng dragged him out, and William Kylter and Pascoe Trevian stabbed him to death. Two days of rioting followed, until the Justices of the Peace rounded up the ringleaders. The Kylters, Trevian and six others were convicted of treason, and were hanged at Launceston, their entrails removed and burnt, their heads cut off and bodies quartered. Geffrey suffered the same fate at Smithfield. Cornwall smouldered for a year, then erupted into the 1549 Prayerbook Rebellion in which some 5,000 rebels were killed or executed. The introduction of the English Prayerbook led to the decline in the use of the Cornish language.

◀ Constantine's band – originally part of the Ist Battalion DCI Volunteers – have been accompanying village events from at least the 1850s. During the 20th century the band's fortunes waxed and waned, due to wars, lack of money or lack of interest. The present incarnation has been doing well since 1977, winning prizes, performing abroad and receiving a large lottery grant in 1998 for buying new instruments. They've been blowing their own trumpets ever since.

Features: *Constantine church and village; the hamlets of Brill, Brillwater and Bridge; the secrets of Brill Hill and Glebe Gardens.*
Terrain: *fields muddy in winter; some road walking.*
Duration: *1 – 2 hours.*

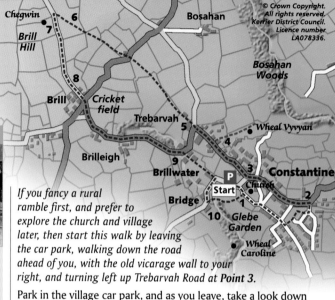

The village school

Before the 1870s, village girls and boys both attended the British School at Ponjeravah *(see page 16)* where, in 1850, it was reported that about 80 pupils of each sex attended. The Church of England school for girls (and boys aged under 7) was built in 1864 – facilities were limited at first, books were scarce, and there was little in the way of organised sporting activities.

Above, dinner time in the 1930s.

The old vicarage in the 1900s. In 1726 it was described as 'very ancient, of stone covered with thatch'. There was also a malthouse, kiln, barn, stable and three gardens. The Glebe (see page 10) comprised 5 acres of arable fields and 60 ash, oak and elm trees 'of little value'. The vicar received a tithe of 'fish, coppice-wood, honey, hops and apples [and] one lamb in seven'.

Lower Fore Street in the 1900s. The girl is sitting on a mounting block outside the preacher's stable, beside the former methodist chapel. ▶

*If you fancy a rural ramble first, and prefer to explore the church and village later, then start this walk by leaving the car park, walking down the road ahead of you, with the old vicarage wall to your right, and turning left up Trebarvah Road at **Point 3**.*

Park in the village car park, and as you leave, take a look down Vicarage Terrace to your left at the church hall, just behind the public toilets – for almost a century this was the village school for girls and infants, until the new school was built in 1964.

1 St Constantine's church

Turn right in front of the former vicarage – this replaced an earlier vicarage *(pictured left)* on Vicarage Terrace, demolished to make an entrance to the recreation ground. Walk down the road towards the church, its 100ft tower standing high for 550 years; climb the steps to explore the church, otherwise continue down the road between the churchyards, and ahead into Bowling Green lane. The building just before the WI Hall on your right was the telephone exchange, while the one after, Tean, was the police house in the 1950s. About 20m after Parc Monga on your right, take the path on your left, following it as it curves round and turn left at the first junction. Turn right after 80m and walk down to Penbothidno road; turn left, and you'll arrive at Fore Street.

St Constantine's church & churchyard

Christians have been worshipping here for 1500 years, first in the Celtic monastery dedicated to St Constantine *(page 4)*; then in a Norman church; and from the 15th century in the present church, erected of local granite with an impressive double-buttressed tower. The chancel was rebuilt in 1862, and in 1901 the walls scraped of their plaster, including any remaining medieval murals – just a fragment survives in the Bosahan aisle. The first vicar, Nicholas, was appointed in 1286, and was later part of a gang of clerics who assaulted and nearly killed the Dean of St Buryan. In 1875 vicar Robert Rickards, whilst inspecting repairs on the church roof, slipped and fell, sustaining fatal injuries.

Look for the beautiful carvings on the parish chest and the remains of the rood screen; the outstanding tapestry kneelers (over 300 of them!); the monumental brasses (one possibly the oldest in Cornwall); the 1973 Lady Chapel window, depicting a Cornish chough and St Constantine; and the stone heads at the foot of the west door *(right)*.

Beside the church, next to the lych gate, is the parish vestry. In 1785 its ground floor was Constantine's first school, taught by Oliver Granville on a salary of £10 a year; within two months he'd been dismissed. In the eastern corner of the churchyard *(above)* you'll find a granite monument to William Bishop, lost at sea in the sinking of the *SS Lusitania* in 1915, and close by a memorial to James Veal who went down with the *Titanic*, 1912.

2 Fore Street

Turn left up Fore Street, opposite Hodges' butchers. From the late 19th century, 4 Fore Street was Noble's General Store selling tobacco, ginger ale and chips on Saturday nights. Further up on the left you'll pass a old garage, now a charity shop; in the 1930s the daily bus which took village workers to Falmouth Docks was kept here. Little Stone was once a carpenter's shop, as was Constantine Stores – now famous for its selection of wines and spirits (including more than 700 whiskies!). Look for the waterspout on the left, one of several supplying the village from the 1880s *(page 8)*. The building opposite was the preacher's stable, and the methodist chapel next door is now the Tolmen Centre *(page 2)*, the centre of village life and venue for lectures, concerts and plays; it has a fascinating museum and a café.

35 Fore Street was the first police house and from the late 19th century, 40 was the Post & Telegraph Office. The white house two doors up from the PO was Grace Symond's store in the early 1900s and Johnnie Tremayne's shop in the 1930s. The Bow Window – now an information centre offering internet access – was once the house of Charlie Bishop the blacksmith; his smithy was situated behind numbers 41 and 43.

Further up you pass the Queen's Arms; a century ago this was the Cornish Arms, and the white building opposite was the original Queen's Arms in the days when the village's mining and quarrying industry could support two pubs. Beyond the pub, the electrical stores was previously a cobblers, a bakery and a greengrocery, and in Church Square, Frank Eddy's cobbler's hut was once where the Spar shop now stands; in 1873, the village kept four shoe-makers busy! On your left, opposite the Spar, the Medlyn family butchers traded for decades from the 1880s until they shut up shop in the early 1950s.

3 Trebarvah Road

Cross over the road; the new paved area, with its tiled murals, is one of many recent improvements – the granite posts represent the four thatched cottages of Bank Terrace, demolished here in

Noble's general store in the 1920s

Post & Telegraph Office in the 1920s

Symond's store in the 1900s

Bank Terrace, now demolished

Constantine AFC in 1933, at the end of a successful season in which they carried off both the Goodman and Lockhart league cups.

Water

When Constantine's wells were no longer adequate for its growing population, a spring at Trebarvah was chosen as a supply. The water ran along 6" pipes through Brillwater, Bridge Hill and into the village, where taps were installed at intervals – you'll see some on Vicarage Terrace, Fore Street and Well Lane. In 1884 the vicar visited Ponjeravah School and exhorted the boys not to *'meddle with the taps of the newly-constructed waterworks'.*

Trebarvah school

The daughters of farmer Walter Row must have seemed quite radical for 1920s Constantine.

Miss Lydia ran the Trebarvah Boarding School, teaching 'house wifery and practical open-air work' to girls aged 7 to 21, with a few places for boys under 10 year's old. Boasting 'house modern, situation healthy, climate equable', she followed the latest in educational theories, the pupil-centred Dalton Laboratory Plan, introduced by American reformer Helen Pankhurst in 1919.

Meanwhile, Miss Ann worked as a nurse and masseuse from Trebarvah, offering 'Massage Electricity, Ling's Medical Exercises, Schott-Nauheim and Weir-Mitchell treatments".

the 1950s to widen the road. Continue up Trebarvah Road, and soon you'll pass the Constantine Social Club on your left, built with a legacy from Alice Hext of Trebah, a great benefactor of the village. The small building with wooden doors, after the Social Club, once housed the bier, the carriage for carrying coffins. Further up the road, you'll pass Wheal Vyvyan estate on your right, with the mine chimney visible above the rooftops.

Cross over the road and walk past the recreation field, another legacy of Alice Hext. The field was later extended, with further improvements in 1997. The dishes of Goonhilly and the wind turbines of Bonython are visible from here. On your right is the site of Ruberry's garage, closed in 1994. The ground here is riddled with mine workings.

4 Detour to Wheal Vyvyan chimney stack

A short detour down Trebarvah Lane, past the bungalows on your right, across the stile and along the footpath, will bring you to the chimney of Wheal Vyvyan mine *(see page 18)*.

After the detour, retrace your steps and continue up the road past Trebarvah Close and, on your left, the village primary school, built in 1966 and extensively refurbished in 2005. In 2006 it was voted the best in the county by listeners to local radio station Pirate FM. Buried beneath your feet runs the fibre-optic cable from Goonhilly Earth Satellite Station – the two junction boxes on your left are its markers. On reaching the road junction, notice the handsome signpost, one of many well-preserved posts in the area. In the field on the right, opposite the junction, you can see a dip in the ground, caused by a collapsing mine working – a chamber reputed to be the size of Truro cathedral!

5 Trebarvah

Cross the junction and take the footpath straight ahead through the gate into the old yard of Trebarvah farm. The large house on your left, and the two cottages in the farmyard, were a private boarding school for girls and young boys in the 1920s. Continue through the gate on the far side of the yard, and you'll find yourself in a green lane, hedged with cow parsley and foxgloves, brambles and sloes, ferns, wild strawberries, herb robert, hemp agrimony and hedge woundwort. From the first gap in the hedge you get good views across the fields to the cricket pavilion at Boulder Park, which you'll be passing in a little while. Behind this is Brill Hill, the highest point in the area. A spring in the fields above Trebarvah farm supplied all of Constantine with water from the 1880s until mains water arrived in 1962.

Cross the stile at the top of the path into the field, and keeping the hedge on your right, set a bearing on Chegwidden farmhouse on the skyline ahead. Cross another steep stile after about 150 yards. Bear slightly left across the next field, heading towards the oak tree in front of the electricity sub-station.

Cross the stile onto the road, bear left across the road in front of the sub-station, climb the stile and follow the path to the left of the fence. Pass a hornbeam, a fir and hazel trees and go through a gate. Head straight uphill towards a gate in the hedge, through this and head for the telegraph pole on the horizon.

6 The view from the top field

This viewpoint is a good place to see how Constantine sits within the landscape – Goonhilly satellite dishes to the south; the mound of Dennis Head (just above the hidden Helford River) and Port Navas to the south-east; Falmouth Bay, with Mawnan Smith to the east. In the foreground lies Constantine church, the roof of Trebarvah farm beside it, and Wheal Vyvyan mine-stack to the left.

Climb the stile beside the road, but before you descend, look north-east over to the pile of stones at Retallack Quarry. A century and a half ago the horizon would have been dominated by the distinctive bulk of the Tolmen Stone *(see page 20)*.

7 Chegwin

Turn left along the road, the summit of Brill Hill and its cellphone mast to your right *(see panel)*. On your right, up a track, are the ruins of Chegwin farmhouse – built around 1830 by Robert Trewannick who leased the land from Jane Hill of Carwythenack *(see page 31)*. During the Second World War, this ruin was the first operational base of the Constantine Auxiliary Unit, trained in sabotage and unarmed combat in case of a German invasion. Unfortunately, the local Home Guard accidentally discovered the hideout when they used it for target practice! Continue down the road between high hedges of elder, betony, sheep's-bit, honeysuckle, herb robert and hedge bedstraw. By day you might be accompanied by gatekeeper butterflies; at night, according to local legend, the hoofbeats of 'Lawyer' Scott of Trewardreva *(see page 22)* as he rides his phantom horse and hounds.

8 Brill

Soon you'll be entering the hamlet of Brill – originally *Brehylgh*, and in 1337 part of the Manor of Carwythenack. When you reach the crossroads, go straight ahead, signposted to Constantine and Mawnan Smith. You're now passing the Boulder Parc grounds of the Constantine Cricket Club, bought in 1995 and sporting a new pavilion built in 1997 with lottery funding. The roadside verge at Boulder Parc was, for a while in the 1940s, the site of a primitive air-raid shelter, dug by local villagers and roofed with timber and galvanised iron. Continue downhill past Netherbury – built by Cecil Williams who owned the carpenter's behind it, and grandfather of eminent Cornish historian Philip Payton – and then a cul-de-sac of four houses, one of which is Constantine vicarage.

The secrets of Brill Hill

In a field at the top of Brill Hill was Constantine's very own nuclear bunker. For nine years, until it closed in 1968, this was the secret underground base of the local Royal Observer Corps. A shaft led to a room furnished with canvas chairs, bunk beds and monitoring equipment – meters to measure radioactive fallout and bomb blasts, a pinhole camera to photograph nuclear fireballs, and sirens and maroons to warn the village of missile attacks.

The post was under the command of Vivian Green – at 35 the ROC's youngest ever Area Commandant – who had served with Constantine ROC in World War II, when he was only 16. At that time the role of the ROC was to observe aircraft movements.

Nothing remains of the site today, although you can see similar bunkers, maintained by the National Trust, near Lizard Point *(pictured)* and Nare Head.

Brill Cottage in the early 1900s

Constantine Cricket Club

For over 75 years Constantine's cricket team shared the football pitch on the recreation ground, involving hurried attempts to repair the turf before each summer season. Despite this, the Club established a formidable reputation over the decades. Bob Wyatt, former England captain (and vice-captain during the infamous 'bodyline' tour of Australia in 1932–33) played his last-ever match in the village when, aged nearly 70, he made 20 runs. When the Club moved to Boulder Parc, another test cricketer, Chris Old, officially opened the grounds in 1997.

◀ *The cricket team in the 1930s.*

Brillwater around 1900. Trewardreva, which you walked past at Point 5 and which was later a private school, is in the top right of the picture. This is one of several photographic plates of Constantine and nearby hamlets which were found in an empty attic in Bristol, and which were taken by a Mr Tonkin of Eastleigh, for use as postcards. ▶

Winter heliotrope

Demoiselle damselfly

Wheal Caroline

In 1850, Caroline Scott, daughter of barrister Charles Scott of Trewardreva *(page 22)*, turned the first sod on the mine site that bore her name; six years later the whole enterprise was in ruins.

Wheal Caroline got off to a promising start – by 1854 two shafts had been sunk, an engine house built and pump installed, the mine and level pumped dry and a tin seam quickly discovered. It was then that things started to go wrong: Mr Peters the purser died, work came to a halt, tradesmen's bills were unpaid and the miners went without wages.

By 1856 – the same year that the Scotts sold Trewardreva – the machinery was auctioned off, only raising enough to pay the miners 70% of what they were owed.

9 Brillwater & Bridge

Eventually, at the valley bottom, you reach another hamlet, Brillwater. The stream here runs down to Polpenwith Creek. Turn right down Brillwater Road, heading towards the church tower. The track is pinched into a footpath and then widens again, passing a terrace of houses on your right – built in 1922 this was the first council accommodation in Constantine. You eventually pass the steps up to the recreation ground.

Turn right at the junction – take care, this is a busy road. In a cricket match between Grade Ruan and Constantine in 1985, author Robin Bates hit two consecutive sixes over the fence on your left, losing both balls. Take the footpath on the left, between Bridge Cottage and Paradise Cottage, known as Sentry Lane (from 'Sayntuary Ground' or 'Sanctuarium', as the church lands were known in medieval times) – an ancient cart track into Constantine churchtown. Cross the stream and climb the stile.

10 Glebe Garden

About 10m after the bridge, a gate on the right takes you onto a permissive path around the peaceful oasis of Glebe, or Vicarage, Garden, part of the original church lands and, more recently, the site of an extensive orchard, created by J C Winn who taught orchard-management in the 1940s. Since 1990 the Parish Council, supported by an army of local volunteers, have planted trees, established paths and put up bird boxes, creating a lush wildlife habitat. You might spot dragonflies, great tits and blue tits, nuthatches, treecreepers and woodpeckers flitting over the pools and through the oak, ash, beech and fruit trees, gunnera and tiger lilies. In winter you'll see snowdrops and winter heliotrope, and in spring bluebells, primroses and daffodils.

This tranquil glade was not always thus. A mill catchpool was situated here in the 1850s, with leats running down to the engine house of Wheal Caroline *(see panel)*. There are legends, too, of a secret underground smuggling route leading up to the church; although a well-constructed tunnel does indeed exist – 9m long, braced with huge granite slabs and home to a colony of bats – it's more likely that this is an adit associated with nearby mine shafts.

After exploring the garden, continue up Sentry Path, go through the wooden gate – from here there are views down the valley towards Polwheveral Creek – cross the stile at the top of the path, and return to the car park.

Features: *beautiful countryside, woodland and creekside scenery; an ancient Iron Age settlement; a glimpse inside a Victorian school; overgrown mining ruins.*

Terrain: *some uneven terrain through woodland; short stretch of road-walking; an uphill stretch out of Bosahan Woods. Muddy in places in winter or after rainfall.*

Duration: *1 – 2 hours.*

Starting from Constantine car park, turn right towards the church and then right again, down Back Lane, between the churchyards.

1 Bowling Green road

Continue down Bowling Green (*see page 6*) past Parc Monga on the right, then the doctor's surgery on your right and follow the track straight ahead, past the site of the old bowling green which gives the lane its name. Soon you'll be enjoying rural views over the valley to your right, leading down to Polpenwith Creek. On your left, there are hedges of sloes, montbretia, tutsan and buddleia – a feeding ground for tortoiseshell, cabbage whites and red admirals. After 200 yards, cross over a stile beside a gate, go over the track and cross another stile.

2 The view from the stile

From the top of this stile you're treated to a panoramic rural view. Starting with the parish church behind you, slowly pan to your left, past the white headstones of the new churchyard, then down to the valley at Bridge, with Brill hamlet in the background and Brill Hill topped with its cellphone mast. Move on past Trengilly Farm and Trengilly Wartha Inn in the valley, and the hamlet of Nancenoy; on the horizon the wind turbines at Bonython on the Lizard and Goonhilly satellite dishes; below these, the wooded banks of the Helford River (hidden) and part of Polpenwith Creek. Continue panning left: in the foreground Goongillings farm, then the large fields of Calamansack; ; the distant headland of Dennis Head; the tall pines at High Cross. Finally, continue panning round to the north-east, over Treglidwith farm and Retallack Quarry.

Head downhill across the field towards the gap in the hedge, over the stone stile and straight across the next field towards another gap to the left of the cottage. Go over the steep stile and onto the road opposite Goongillings Orchard.

Map labels: Bosahan, Nanjarrow, Wheelpit, 10, Wheal Nanjarrow, Wheal Vyvyan, Comfort, 11, Mill, Well, Constantine, Ponjeravah, 9, P Start, Church, 1, 2, Polwheveral, Nancenoy, 3, 8, Mills, Trengilly Wartha, Goongillings, Settlement, 4, Iron mine, Polpenwith, 5, 7, Scott's Wood, Polwheveral Creek, Rifle range, 6, Scott's Quay, Polpenwith Creek

Goongillings farm is fully organic and self-sufficient, supplementing its income with holiday cottages. Using traditional techniques of light grazing and late hay cutting, fields are now flower-rich (above), and wildlife habitats preserved. You may see their homebred single-suckled beef cattle, wearing bells, in the fields beside Scott's Wood.

Ancient settlements

Some 2,300 years ago, the hills around Constantine would have been dotted with settlements, each one a bustling community of families and animals, living in thatched roundhouses surrounded by a defensive ditch and rampart. The settlement at Goongillings is just one, well-situated for timber and water, with views over the creeks, and the settlers might also have mined the lode of iron which runs directly beneath the site. There are other earthworks at High Cross and Carwythenack (less well-preserved) and an impressive double enclosure near Merthen Manor *(pictured above)*. Dozens of others are today only identifiable by aerial photography.

3 Goongillings

If you're already in need of refreshments, a short detour to your right, down the sunken lane and over a bridge, brings you to the award-winning Trengilly Wartha Inn; once a farmhouse, and now a freehouse offering an impressive menu.

If you want to leave the delights of the Inn for a while (you'll be passing by this way again later) then cross the road and walk straight up the lane in front of you, hedged with foxgloves, enchanter's nightshade, pennywort, hart's tongue fern, campion, herb robert and clumps of speedwell. At the end of the track climb a stile beneath an ash tree covered in honeysuckle, then continue straight ahead and turn left onto the track heading across the field. Go over another stile beside a gate, with views opening up to distant Goonhilly, and continue to follow the track.

4 Iron Age settlement

In the corner of this field there are two gates. Go through the righthand gate for a short detour to the Iron Age settlement, a scheduled ancient monument overlooking Polpenwith Creek. Follow the hedge on your right, and go through a gap to arrive in a round field, hedged on one side with blackthorn, holly, oak and elder – a pleasant spot to open up the thermos and do some time-travelling. You may hear the plaintive cry of a peacock from Polpenwith. In the wooded valley below the camp are the caves, pits, adits and leats of a late 18th century iron mine – now colonised by greater and lesser horseshoe bats and consequently protected from public access. There were other iron workings across the creek at Calamansack, where Brogden – or Inow – iron mine, with its three shafts and engine house, was operating in the 1870s *(see page 26)*.

Retrace your steps to the gate, and continue down the hedged track. You'll soon come to a barn, built as a hangar to house Captain Dick Pugh's tiny Auster. If you'd passed this way in the mid-1960s, you might have seen young Charlie Pugh (now farmer at Goongillings) swinging the propeller and leaping aside as the engine roared into life, and the plane trundled out into the field to take off over the creek. Nowadays the only flights you're likely to see are made by buzzards, linnets and the odd barn owl.

Continue down the track, dotted with the large-leafed flytraps of lords and ladies, flanked with blackberries and elderberries in autumn, visited by speckled wood butterflies. Go past a lonesome pine, through a gate and over some stepping stones, to arrive at a glade of oak, birch and beech trees.

Goongillings airfield

Ever since he'd been a navy carrier pilot, Capt Dick Pugh had dreamed of one day owning his plane and airstrip. Aged over 60, he retrained for his pilot's licence and in 1963 bought an Auster – just about the smallest aircraft of the time. For the next four years he made breathtaking flights from this tiny field, including one epic journey to Paris to see his daughter, with his brother Jim as navigator.

5 Scott's Wood

To left and right of you is the wood planted by Charles Scott of Trewardreva *(page 22)* in the early 1800s, probably to provide timber for estate and mining use – many of the trees are quick-growing sweet chestnut, favoured by farms for timber. The wood was originally larger; much of it burnt down by two boys in 1911. You'll be exploring this wood later. Continue straight ahead, to emerge into a field, following the track which leads between two granite gateposts; Polpenwith Creek is down on your right. After these gateposts you're walking out onto the promontory between two creeks, with Polwheveral on your left and Polpenwith Creek on your right. This track to the quay was laid down by Scott, and started from Vicarage Terrace, where you began your walk.

Scott's Wood, early 1900s

6 Scott's Quay

Go down the slope, through a gate, and onto the grassy bank of the quay, edged with blackthorn and dog-roses, sprinkled with campion, stitchwort, birdsfoot trefoil, thrift and even the odd early purple orchid. This tranquil spot is perfect for a picnic; the birds think so too – you'll find cracked mussel and cockle shells by the water's edge. If you're a birdwatcher you'll be enjoying a ringside seat, with autumnal displays of migrating turnstones, redshanks, dunlins, curlews and oystercatchers, and year-round sightings of little egrets and herons, which breed around Polwheveral. You might be lucky to spot an occasional kingfisher. Sitting here 150 years ago, you'd have been watching merchant schooners unloading coal and timber onto waiting horse-drawn carts, or taking on board cargoes of quarried stone.

Scott's Quay

'Lawyer' Scott of Trewardreva built the quay in the early 1800s; it originally extended 20m into the creek, allowing schooners to navigate the deep water channel. The quay fell in disrepair with the advent of railways and decline in the mines, and the present, smaller quay was constructed in 1932 by Alice Hext, to encourage public access to the creek.
Above: the quay in the 1900s.

What makes the Helford River so special?

Roman galleys sailing up the Helford River around 1,800 years ago, might well have seen a landscape not so different from that of today – dense woodland of oak, hazel and ash running down to the water's edge, with here and there plumes of smoke from Celtic settlements in clearings or on hilltops. Merthen Woods, on the righthand riverbank as you look down Polwheveral Creek, are so ancient that they are now a Site of Special Scientific Interest.

The Helford River is not really an estuary, but actually a drowned river valley, formed by the rise in sea level after the last Ice Age. It falls within the recently designated Fal & Helford Special Area of Conservation, and is remarkable for its range of habitats – inlets, mudflats and sandbanks – which are home to an astonishing variety of species. Marine biologists get excited about rare fan mussels, and eelgrass and maerl beds, while fishermen respect the oyster fishery and bass nursery. There are anemones, starfish, sea urchins, sea squirts, sponges, lobsters, crabs and cuttlefish – in fact over 80 species of fish have been recorded in the river, including long-snouted sea horses.

To help conserve this rich marine environment, and promote its sustainable use, the Helford Voluntary Marine Conservation Area was set up in 1987, and has been busy working with sailors, fishermen, landowners, biologists, local councils and commercial interests.
You can find out more on **www.helfordmarineconservation.co.uk**

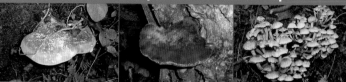

You're bound to find at least one of these species in Scott's Wood, whatever the season. The inedible *Ganoderma applanatum (left)* grows all year round, to widths of 50cm or more. It's known as 'artist's conk' because pictures can be indelibly carved on its underside. *Piptoporus betulinus,* birch fungus, fruits annually on live and dead birch trunks, reducing the wood to a red powder. Also inedible, it was once used to strop razors. The thick red tongues of *Fistulina hepatica,* beefsteak fungus, grow on old oaks, causing decay. The edible flesh drips blood-red juice and tastes acrid. Forming beautiful orange-yellow clusters on dead tree stumps, the poisonous *Hypholoma fasciculare,* or sulphur tuft, can be confused with the edible honey fungus *(page 26)*.

Yellow pimpernel – an astringent herb which can staunch bleeding.

After the war

After World War II, German and Italian prisoners in camps at Mylor and Nansloe Manor, Helston, were bussed out to work on farms around Constantine. Eric Jung and Joseph Burkhart worked for Rose and Manfred Pearce at Trevaney Farm, High Cross, and forged a friendship with the family which survived their repatriation in 1948 and continues to this day.

Polwheveral bridge, 430 years old

Retrace your steps from the Quay, and turn right along the bottom of the field, keeping the creekside hedge to your right – be careful not to step into one of the many ankle-breaking badger holes. In the field corner go through the narrow gap in the fence and take the path into the wood, following the trail of white spots painted on the trunks, keeping an eye out for low-slung branches and slippery mud. As the path continues along the top of the creek bank, through oak, holly, birch, beech and chestnut trees, in late summer you'll catch glimpses of the yellow gorse and purple heathclad slopes of Calamansack across the water.

7 Neumann's Tree

As the path swings away from the creek, look out for a tree, multi-trunked and with mossy green socks, carved with the name of Neumann, dated 1946 – he was a German prisoner-of-war working at Goongillings farm. Continue to follow the white spots, walking on a carpet of beech nuts past clumps of yellow pimpernel. The path eventually follows a line of beech along the edge of the field. Keep an ear cocked for the sounds of woodpeckers, and you may come across the debris of a squirrel's picnic – spruce cones stripped of their seed scales. Go through a wooden gate to arrive back at Point 5. Turn right up the track, past the hangar barn, and retrace your steps to reach the road at Point 3. Turn right down the hill; this is an old cart-track leading to Polwheveral Mill, lined with ferns, pennywort and primroses.

8 Polwheveral

At the bottom of the slope you'll be passing Lower Goongillings Cottage, where fragments of jugs and cooking pots dating back to the 13th century – and storage jars and cisterns 200 or 300 years older – have been found in the grounds. There is also a granite mouldstone in the cottage yard, probably from the smelting house situated just across the river in the early 19th century.

You're 260 miles from London here, as a granite milestone opposite the cottage informs you, and you're walking along one of the principal medieval routes of the parish, stretching from Mawnan Smith and Penryn, all the way to Helston, where tin ingots carried by carts along this route would have been weighed and valued at the Coinage Hall.

Walk over the old bridge, virtually unchanged since mason Roger Hallard first built it in 1572 for £3 6s 8d, according to the contract recorded in the parish vestry book. Pass over the low bank into the field on your right, directly after the bridge. You're now on an attractive permissive path around the head of the creek through the gardens of Mill House, and an ideal spot for unwrapping the sandwiches. The banks at the head of the creek are known as the Saltings; it's thought that a dam (known locally as the Ramshire) enabled the creek to be used as a salt bed, and the collected salt was taken to the cellars at Frenchman's Creek.

After your detour to the creek, retrace your steps to the bridge and cross straight over the road into the small meadow beyond. You're now following another permissive path, keeping the fern-lined banks of the stream on your left until you pass through a gap in the field boundary, passing large hydrangeas and into woodland. Walk up the slope to reach a T-junction in the path, turn right and go back on yourself for about 20m, then turn left uphill along the bridleway through Polwheveral Woods. This track was the main route to the Polwheveral mills from Constantine, and down on your left would have been the mill pool which fed the leat running down to the grist mills.

After 150 yards or so you'll pass the sewage treatment works. When you reach the farm track, leading to Polwheveral House Farm, turn left and continue along the lane edged with sycamore, oak, cherry and lime trees, and populated by badgers, speckled wood butterflies and beautiful demoiselles. Eventually you'll reach the main Falmouth to Constantine Road. Cross over and turn left down to the bridge, passing the building which was home to Ponjeravah School (see page 16), then afterwards Constantine Youth Club, and is now a handsome house.

(see page 16)

Life in Polwheveral

Jack Williams (above left, aged 5), who lived in what is now Creek Cottage, paints a vivid picture of Polwheveral life in the 1930s. The small community was almost self-sufficient: his father, a boatman, caught fish and shot pigeon and rabbit; milk, butter and eggs came from his grandparents' farm at the Elms (Mill House); vegetables and fruit from the gardens. Farmer Bill Trethowan had the only car in the valley (an old American model) while the sole wireless belonged to Mr Roberts at Polwheveral Cottage, where the neighbours would gather 'to hear important things such as boxing matches'.

Cadets at the rifle range, 1943

Shooting, stamping and grinding – peaceful Polwheveral in the past

The beautiful backwater of Polwheveral is more peaceful now than at many times in its past. Around 60 years ago, the creek echoed with the crack of rifle fire, as the home guard, cadets and soldiers practised on the firing range which ran for 800 yards along the eastern bank of the creek. Built in the late 19th century, and used by the local Volunteers, the crumbling remains of the target butts can still be seen beneath the trees at low tide.

A century earlier, when Wheal Vyvyan and Wheal Nanjarrow were at full stretch in the 1840s, the noise from Polwheveral's stamping mill would have been deafening. The stamps employed about 10 men and boys, and the crushed copper was transported to South Wales for smelting. The smaller *Polwheveral's mills*

amount of tin would have been heated in the charcoal-fired furnace in the smelting house just below the mill, then poured into granite moulds for ingots. Quantities of the resulting 'tap slag' have been recovered from the creekside meadows. Polwheveral's two grist mills were still working around this time, grinding corn as they had been since medieval times. By the 1890s they were no longer used although they are still standing today – Creek Cottage and Mill House. In the 17th century there was also a 'tucking' or 'fulling' mill for weaving homespun cloth, run by the Mayne family.

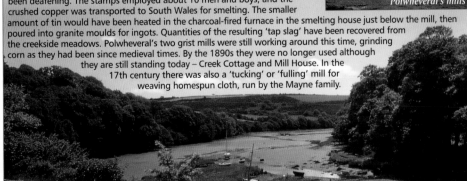

The Ponjeravah 'academy'

'Nicholas Evans pushed S Rowlin over the bridge in the river during the dinnertime' reads an 1874 entry from the Ponjeravah School headmaster's logbook. Other remarks complain of 'defective' buildings, truancy, boys cheating at marbles and smoking pipes.

The school was built in 1836, due largely to the efforts of Charles Fox of Trebah, and followed the Lancaster system of using monitors to teach younger children. Girls attended until the village school opened in 1864 *(page 6)*, and weekly fees (one to three pence) were paid until free education was introduced in 1891. Alterations were carried out in 1908 and 1913; electricity (and radio) arrived in 1949; and the playground was surfaced the following year. In 1951 children from both schools visited London for the Festival of Britain, and again in 1953 for Coronation Week. Ponjeravah School closed in 1964, when the new Constantine School was completed. *Pictured: the school in 1921, headmaster R Dunn on the left.*

The Nanjarrow hermit

For almost 40 years, William Rowe was concealed by his family at Nanjarrow Farm, after he had deserted during the First World War. The village assumed that he had been killed in action, and it was not until an amnesty was declared by Queen Elizabeth II that he emerged from hiding. Sadly, Rowe was to die again in 1963, killed by burglars hunting for the money which it was believed that he had stashed away.

Ponsamayo Bridge

▲ *The Tredwen sisters farmed at Comfort in the mid-20th century, and were often seen herding their cows along Fore Street, taking them home for milking from their pastures at the bottom of the village.*

Comfort in the early 1900s, as seen from Well Lane near the water tap. The terraced cottages are still there, but the bungalows of Comfort Wartha now stand where there was once a row of miners' cottages. ▶

9 Ponjeravah Bridge

If you want a quick route back to Constantine, follow the road up the hill (a busy road), otherwise turn right and follow the public bridleway, keeping the riverbanks, dotted with wood sorrel and bugle, on your left. After 200m you'll see Manor Mill (once Churchtown Mill) across the river; the Ponjeravah stamps were also sited on this stream in the first half of the 18th century, employing some 20 men and boys. Pass through the two tall granite gateposts to Nanjarrow Farm, and keep on up the incline; beneath the brambles to the right are the shaft and adit of Wheal Nanjarrow, a small copper mine which operated here up to 1857.

10 Ponsamayo bridge

After about 10 minutes, you'll reach a waymarker; turn left here into Bosahan Woods, and a glade of pools and mossy boulders. Go over Ponsamayo Bridge and on your right is the enormous wheel pit of Wheal Vyvyan mine *(see page 18)*. Head up the old cart-track, passing more mine ruins on the slopes above you. Swing to the right at the top, follow the track then turn left – straight ahead is Wheal Vyvyan chimney stack. Head left along the narrow path, down some steps, and turn right onto Well Lane.

11 Comfort

Continue along the lane and up the slope, through the hamlet of Comfort. A grassy footpath on the left, between two gardens, leads to one of the wells which supplied the village until the water-points were installed in the 1870s. Continue along Well lane to reach Fore Street, and turn right, passing the paved area where the Bank Terrace cottages once stood, past the Spar, and turn left on to Vicarage Terrace and back to your starting point.

Features: a walk through Constantine's industrial past; the mine workings of Bosahan Woods; disused quarries and the site of the Tolmen Stone; a prehistoric underground refuge; historic houses and farms; lush meadows, panoramic views.
Terrain: some uneven terrain through Bosahan Wood & Quarry; muddy stretches in winter.
Duration: 2 – 3 hours, depending on detours.

Leave your car in the village car park and walk along the road ahead of you, keeping the church on your right behind the vicarage wall. At the junction, turn right, then left along Well Lane, opposite the Spar stores.

1 Well Lane

Continue down the lane, passing the grassy path which leads down to one of the village wells, until you eventually turn left onto a public footpath and climb some granite steps, just after Comfort Farm *(see page 16).*

2 Wheal Vyvyan

Over on your left, across a field, stands the engine house stack of Wheal Vyvyan mine, *(see page 18)* and Dennis' Shaft (collared with a Cornish hedge). When you reach a junction of paths beside a wooden gate, turn right and follow the path as it curves round a garden wall and a large ivy bush, in late summer festooned with red admirals; the area of bracken and brambles to your left used to be the water pound for the mine.

The path descends beneath oak trees, past a clump of Japanese knotweed on your right, and as you enter the woods there are the remains of Wheal Fire mine shaft which was capped with concrete by the villagers on a single Saturday afternoon in 1985.

Continue down the beech-shaded incline; you're walking along an old cart-track, and 150 years ago you'd have been elbowed aside by carts carrying dressed copper ore up from the valley floor. The ivy-covered ruins of wheel pits and other buildings litter the slopes of the bank on your left, and at the bottom you'll see the largest wheel pit, which once carried a 42ft diameter wheel, and hauled ore trucks up an incline shaft joined to Dennis' Adit.

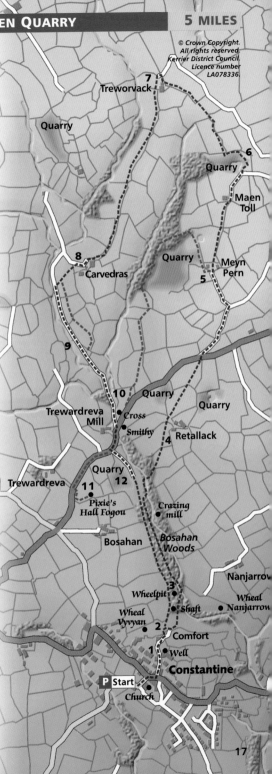

Wheal Vyvyan – when copper was king

Wheal Vyvyan was the largest mine in Constantine, and the village's fortunes in the 19th century depended on it. In 1801 the parish population was 1,229, and the churchtown was a hamlet of some 20 houses; fifty years later, at the height of the copper boom, the population had increased by 70% to 2,093, and new miners' cottages marched down Fore Street and along Well Lane.

Copper and tin had been mined here before 1827, but it was after this date that the mine really got going, under the ownership of Sir Richard Vyvyan of Trelowarren. Between 1818 and 1856 the mine extracted 8,277 tons of copper ore (producing 500 tons of copper) and in one year alone, 20 tons of tin. Four new shafts had been sunk, and the workforce included 80 miners underground, 30 men and boys at the Ponjeravah and Polwheveral stamps *(pages 15 & 16)*, and a dozen bal-maidens for hand-breaking the ore.

The mine workings extended from Western Shaft, just west of Trebarvah Road, to the shafts and adits east of the Ponjeravah stream at Ponsamayo. Like all Cornish mines, Wheal Vyvyan depended on water power – water wheels drove the ranks of piledrivers (**stamps**) which crushed the ore, and the largest wheel hauled ore-laden trucks up the incline railway which led into Dennis' Shaft. All these wheels were fed by channels, or **leats**, which ran from water pounds or from further upstream at Trewardreva Mill.

In 1857 a steam engine was built, the chimney of which still stands, to help pump the mine dry, but by this time the mine was already in decline; only 200 tons of ore (copper and tin) were produced from 1857 to 1864, a fraction of the mine's production before 1850. This coincided with the flood of cheap copper from Michigan and Chile. Cornwall's reign as 'king of copper' was over.

The human cost of copper

According to coroners' reports, during a seven-month period in the 1830s, the mine suffered more than its fair share of accidents. In September 1836, 21-year-old John Grigg was blowing rocks at the 20-fathom level west of Rowse's shaft when a three-ton boulder fell on him *'and nearly cut him in two. The poor fellow lived about five minutes'*. In February 1837, George James, a stamps boy, *'was accidentally jammed by a crank attached to the axis of the stamp wheel, and killed on the spot'*; George was only 12 years old, and would have been earning about £1 a month. On April 5th, William Tresidder, on his way *'back to grass'* from the 20-fathom level west of old engine shaft, stepped on *'a loose pile of stuff'*, fell five fathoms and *'being loaded with heavy bars of iron at the time, was so much injured that he died'*.

Enchanter's nightshade

The remains of a late-medieval crazing mill on the eastern slopes. A blowing house – 'molendinum sufflaticum – was recorded here in 1506, and millstones, wheelpits and mould stones have been found.

3 Bosahan Woods – the bluebell wood

You've now reached the shaded valley bottom of Bosahan Woods, a tranquil spot which belies its industrial past. About 150 years ago the valley would have been bereft of trees, and busy with women and boys spalling (breaking) the ore with hammers, and men carrying the copper nuggets by barrow or cart down to the Ponjeravah stamps. The deafening clatter of the stamps would compete with the steady clank and rumble of the huge 42ft wheel, as it pulled ore wagons up the incline shaft, and the slopes would be threaded with leats feeding water to the mill wheels.

Cross over the granite bridge of Ponsamayo, and then the stile, continuing along the riverside and over a wooden bridge. The path veers left past brambles and ferns, then begins its ascent through the woods; in spring you'll realise why the locals call this the Bluebell Wood. Sixty years ago you'd have been walking through waist-high '*brouse*' (bracken and brambles) after most of the beech trees had been felled in 1945 for timber; today's woodland has been self-sown from the few trees left standing. To the left you'll see the mossy banks of medieval field boundaries; to your right, across the river and beneath the fallen trees and undergrowth, are the ruins of crazing mills and blowing houses – a 15th and 16th century tin-dressing complex.

Follow the path to eventually turn right beside a huge pile of moss-covered granite, a spoil heap from Bosahan Quarry (see page 22). The path wends past clumps of wood-sorrel and ferns, crosses an ancient granite bridge, and climbs the valley side, its banks edged with betony, herb robert and polypody. Climb some granite steps and enter a field. Bear left and head towards the chimneys of Retallack farmhouse, sidestepping a boulder to the right of the path. Keep an eye on the skies for circling buzzards.

4 Retallack

Cross a granite stile. Across the valley on our left we can see the handsome Trewardreva manor, while below it to the right is the former Trewardreva Mill. The spoil heap, right, is Trewardreva Vean Quarry, and on the horizon is Brill Hill cellphone mast and the 1980s experimental wind generator. Keeping the house to your right, head up across the field towards the corner. Looking westwards, you'll see the Bosahan Quarry – the blocks of granite we passed earlier came from there. Looking south, you can pick out the Constantine church tower and Goonhilly satellite dishes behind it. Go over a granite stile into a glade, carpeted in spring with yellow archangel, then over another stile and on your right is a crop of the invasive vanilla-scented winter heliotrope.

Cross the track which leads to Retallack farm and go over another stile; you're on an ancient path leading to Maen Quarry – and eventually to the Halfway House inn at Rame. Follow the path across a field of young trees, including laurel, alder, oak and ash. Keep your eyes peeled for speedwell, greater birdsfoot trefoil and early purple orchids. Over on your right lies a stone circle folly and beyond the field, the spoil heap of Retallack quarry.

Climb another stile into a field, head for the gate and stile in the corner, then go straight across the road onto the bridlway opposite, leading up towards Meyn Pern farm. Follow the track, bordered with scabious, yarrow, goldenrod and hedge bedstraw, and eventually it becomes a concrete path and curves to the left. Pause and take in the views over the gate on your right, out to Mawnan Smith and the sea beyond. Standing here on 20 July 1588, you'd have seen the Spanish Armada approaching Falmouth.

5 Meyn Pern & Maen Toll

Follow the track into Meyn Pern farmyard and turn down to the right after the house, keeping the barn to your left (for a shorter walk, through some old quarries, follow the permissive path to the left of the barn – see panel). Turn left after the barn and climb a stile into the field behind. This farm, and its neighbour Maen Toll, date back to medieval times and were named after the great stones dominating their lands (maen is Cornish for 'rock'). Cornwall's largest menhir once stood at Meyn Pern – 7.5m high, 3m round and embedded over 1m in the ground – until in 1764 the farmer decided it would be more use sliced up into gateposts.

Taking care on the uneven ground, cross the field, following the Cornish hedge, partly made from enormous granite boulders cleared from the fields. Climb over the stile in the corner of the field, follow the hedge on your right, and cross a further three stiles through glades to arrive behind the buildings of Maen Toll.

Retallack Farm

Retallack probably takes its name from Cornish 'res' and 'talek' meaning 'ford near a high slope' referring to the granite slab bridge you passed over. There has probably been a farm at Retallack since the Middle Ages, and during Tudor times it was part of the Manor of Merthen, leased by Nicholas Pentacost; remnants of his mansion can be seen in the farm's stone arches of Norman and Gothic design. The farmland included the late medieval tin-dressing works in the valley.

Hedge woundwort – like yellow pimpernel (p 14) its leaves contain antiseptic oils used to treat wounds

Retallack Gate quarrymen, 1929

Quarry diversion

This permissive path starts at Meyn Pern farmyard, passes to the left of the barn, through a wooden gate and into a grassy lane. Follow the lane through some impressive quarry workings, then downhill through four fields, with spectacular views, to arrive in 25 minutes on the B3291 near Trewardreva Mill at **Point 10**. *Note: can be very wet in winter.*

The Tolmen Stone

Dominating the skyline for miles, and a popular attraction for Victorian excursionists, the Tolmen Stone was a gigantic granite pebble – 10m long, 4.5m high, weighing some 750 tons – which balanced on two smaller rocks, overhanging a working quarry. Quarry workers were experiencing difficult times, with many emigrating to America, and Maen Quarry foreman John Dunstan was anxious to get at the bed of valuable granite beneath the stone.

For five days, despite the gathering angry crowds, the quarrymen undermined the rock by drilling and blasting, until finally on 9 March 1869, as reported by the *West Briton*: '*this ancient colossal monument slowly swerved and majestically slid to the bottom of the quarry. A deep feeling of grief and regret... pervades the district'*. Days later, quarrymen were seen on the Helston to Penryn roadside selling souvenir chunks of the Tolmen for just a few pence.

This act of '*Gothic barbarism'* so appalled geologists and antiquarians that within weeks it led to the founding of a committee for the Preservation of Ancient Monuments, and in 1882, the Ancient Monuments Protection Act.

Maen Quarry

Hedge brown, or gatekeeper

Treworvack

Legend has it that Treworvack was rebuilt in 1600 with granite from Penryn's Glasney College, after the dissolution of the monasteries, but it's more likely that the stone came from a chapel that once stood here. John Tremayne, tenant farmer in 1721, probably added the Gothic porch and gateway – his initials are carved above the arch. In 1589 farmer Thomas Robert was appointed as tithingman for the Tucoys Manor, responsible for bringing felons to court – a sort of medieval Neighbourhood Watch.

6 Maen Quarry

Walk to the right around the house to arrive beside the farmyard, facing the huge rock once known locally as the Devil's Night-cap. Continue up the drive and after 50m, when the concrete track swings round to the right, carry straight ahead onto a grassy path.

After about 80m you'll be overlooking Maen Quarry and its pond – home to newts, toads, damselflies and dragonflies – and you're standing on the spot where the Tolmen Stone once stood, just left of the path. Go around the lip of the quarry and down the path edged with foxgloves and willowherb. After 100m, before two gates, follow the path left between blackthorn and brambles. Turn right (opposite the 'private' sign) and climb the stile beside the gate into the fields of Treworvack farm. You're about to cross the boundary into the ancient Manor of Tucoys, the only Constantine parish manor named in the 1085 Domesday survey.

Follow the hedge on your right and after 150m head through the gate – a mudbath in winter! – and follow the hedge on your left, down the incline towards the corner. Climb the stile beneath a hawthorn tree, then proceed straight ahead towards a gate; go through the gate and follow the hedge on the left. Continue on towards a metal gate; go through this and turn left onto the road.

7 Treworvack

Enter the attractive farmyard of Treworvack, lined with old stables and outhouses. Go through the yard, keeping the house on your left, and as you pass the pillared gateway, take a peek at the handsome porch. Leave the yard through the two sets of double gates, turn right, then immediately left after the wooden barns, and follow the gorse hedge on your left, along the top of the field.

Continue heading towards the distant mast on the horizon, above the wooded valley. Cross the stile in the corner and keep following the hedge, through this field and the next, and then through a gateway with granite posts. Leave the next field through another gate in the corner, and into an old cart track hedged with campion, brambles and blackthorn. On a summer's day this green lane is busy with butterfly traffic – speckled woods, red admirals and tortoiseshells. When the path levels out, look over the gate on your left for a good view of Maen Quarry.

8 Carvedras

Go through a gate into Carvedras farm, and take the path straight ahead, keeping the barn on your right, and then through another gate and follow the track. The farm holding over to your left is Little Carvedras and in 1318, when the land was known as *Kearweddros Parva*, Nicholas Daunte paid a rent of a pair of white gloves and a pair of white spurs to the Lord of Reskymer. When you meet another track, go straight ahead, through the gate and into a field. Make your way down the slope through the young trees, heading for the stile which you'll see as you descend the hill (if you prefer, you can take a permissive path through the fields on your left, past a new pond, to join the track further down the valley). Climb the stile and turn left down the track.

Yellow rattle

9 Carvedras Bottoms

Continue along the track, which in summer runs beside damp meadows teeming with wild flowers – swathes of ragged robin and sorrel, interspersed with buttercups, spear thistles, lady's smock, birdsfoot trefoil, yellow rattle and tall foxgloves. Further down the valley, you'll find spectacular displays of early purple and marsh orchids; attempts are being made to stop the spread of Himalayan balsam along the stream. Above the trees on your right is the rock pile of Trewardreva Vean Quarry. Keep an eye on the sky too – for buzzards, kestrels, sparrowhawks and hen harriers; snipe and woodcock in winter; and barn owls at dusk.

Southern marsh orchids

10 Trewardreva Mill

Passing over a cattle grid, the track enters a glade, with a huge pile of quarry spoil on the right. About 100m after the grid you'll pass the remains of a granite bridge, washed away in the floods of January 2003. As you approach the old buildings of Trewardreva Mill, the line of trees across the field on your right marks the course of the mill leat. The track emerges onto a road; the building in front of you was once a smithy, and one of the area's medieval stone crosses *(see page 25)* is 50m to your left. Turn right up the road, over the stream and continue uphill until you reach the road on your left leading to Bosahan Quarry.

Trewardreva Mill

In feudal times, the Lord of the Manor owned the local mill, and tenants had no choice but to grind their corn there. Millers exacted a toll – a percentage of the barley – and were frequently dishonest. Trewardreva Mill was the mill of Polwheveral Manor, and was still working in 1914 when the miller was William Henry Jenkin. None of the mill fittings remains today.

11 Detour to Piskey's Hall fogou

If you want to head straight back to the village, then turn left here, but if you want to explore the mysterious Piskey's Hall fogou, take a 400m detour up the road until you reach the granite pillars which guard the entrance to Trewardreva house *(see page 22)*. Go through the gate opposite and follow the permissive path around the edge of Piskey Field (a corruption of the original name *Parc-an-Pascoes* – the fattening field) to arrive at the fogou.

This underground stone passageway, 7m long and roofed with granite slabs, is similar to that found at Halligye, Trelowarren, across the Helford River. Dating back 2000 years to the Iron Age, such fogous (Cornish for 'caves') might have been built for ritual purposes, as places of refuge, or for storing perishables (during World War II, Halligye was used by the Manaccan secret auxiliary unit for hiding explosives). Afterwards, return to the road, retrace your steps downhill, then turn right on to the quarry driveway.

Trewardreva stone cross

Piskey's Hall fogou

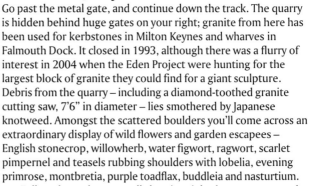
Trewardreva in 1930s

The fortunes of Trewardreva have ebbed and flowed over the years. The lands were owned first by the church, then seized after the Norman Conquest by the Lord of Cornwall, Robert de Montain; by 1086 they were held by Wihurmarc the Breton, Lord of Tucoys. By the 13th century the lands were part of the Manor of Polwheveral, and by 1570 Trewardreva was the manor house of Polwheveral.

Let's pay a visit to Trewardreva in 1600. Wealthy landowner Thomas Rise, steward to the Manor of Tucoys, is putting the finishing touches to his Elizabethan mansion, erecting the coat of arms that will still be seen above the porch some four centuries later. If we drop by in 1719, we find the builders are at it again; Rise's descendant Thomas Trewren and his wife Alice are giving the house a makeover – out go those dreary mullioned windows, in come the trendy Queen Anne sashes. They've added some 18th century decking – a parapet with stone vases – and titivated the rooms with fine plaster ceilings and panelling.

A century later, and things are not so rosy. Thomas and Alice's grandson, a sea captain, has moved away and disinherited his only son, and the estate – including Polwheveral, Goongillings and Carvedras, together with mines and quarries – is now in the hands of his son-in-law, Charles Scott. A Falmouth barrister with extravagant tastes,

Trewardreva in the 17th century

Courtesy of the Hearle family

Scott establishes the quay and woods at Polwheveral, but leaves his eldest son with debts so huge that he will have to sell the estate to repay them. In 1863 we find the builders are busy once more, demolishing half the house for the new owner Mr Hearle, the former estate mason, who thriftily recycles the stone to build new cottages at Trewardreva Cross.

When we call in 1936, the house is dilapidated and the roof full of holes; but the builders are already at work repairing the damage and adding an east wing for the new owner, Romney Fox. Our last visit is in 1986, when we're greeted with the shout *'Quiet on set!' and* the cameras start to roll for an episode of Sherlock Holmes – *The Devil's Foot* – starring Jeremy Brett.

12 Bosahan Quarry

Go past the metal gate, and continue down the track. The quarry is hidden behind huge gates on your right; granite from here has been used for kerbstones in Milton Keynes and wharves in Falmouth Dock. It closed in 1993, although there was a flurry of interest in 2004 when the Eden Project were hunting for the largest block of granite they could find for a giant sculpture. Debris from the quarry – including a diamond-toothed granite cutting saw, 7'6" in diameter – lies smothered by Japanese knotweed. Amongst the scattered boulders you'll come across an extraordinary display of wild flowers and garden escapees – English stonecrop, willowherb, water figwort, ragwort, scarlet pimpernel and teasels rubbing shoulders with lobelia, evening primrose, montbretia, purple toadflax, buddleia and nasturtium.

Bosahan quarrymen & tools, 1900s

Follow the path, eventually bearing right down a grassy path beneath overhanging trees (paths off to your left lead to more spoil heaps and views over Bosahan Woods). The path continues downhill, becoming a stony track as it enters Bosahan Woods beside an ancient granite stile. Take the upper path through the woods (the left fork takes you down to the path you were on at Point 2), noticing just to your left a shallow fern-fringed ditch which runs parallel to the path. This is a leat which ran from upstream near Trewardreva Mill, supplying water to the water pound at Wheal Vyvyan, which you passed at Point 2 *(page 17)*.

Granite saw blade at Bosahan

Continue along the top path as it sidesteps the occasional granite boulders and passes the earthworks of large badger setts. Finally you'll leave the woods and re-emerge to join the path junction at Point 2. Take the right-hand path towards the village, leading you down to Well Lane and Comfort Farm *(page 16)*.

Evening primrose

Constantine Granite – providing the building blocks of Victorian Britain

Bosahan Quarry in the 1920s, with the steam traction engine 'Alpha'; early quarry cranes were driven by hand or horse. Holes were originally drilled with iron 'jumpers' struck with sledge-hammers; these were later replaced by steel drills, and in the mid-20th century, pneumatic drills.

If you take a trip down the Thames from the centre of London, you'll pass walls and piers of stone – London Bridge, Tower Bridge, Woolwich Dockyard – hewn from the hills around Constantine and shipped out from Port Navas *(page 27)*.

Granite 'moorstone', hauled from hilltop outcrops, had been used for building since prehistoric times, but it wasn't until the early 19th century that quarrying became big business, as cities throughout the country began throwing up new buildings, bridges and statues, and edging their pavements with granite kerbs. Soon Constantine's hills and valleys were being gouged for granite, and quarrying became as important to the village as mining.

The quarries worked on a 'piecework' basis, with teams of men working for a 'ganger' who would negotiate a contract with the quarry owner for each granite block; when the stone was finished, the agreed price would then be divided amongst the men according to their individual rates. But it was an uncertain trade – quarries prospered in the late 19th century, but lost out to foreign competition in the early 1900s. The industry revived again after both World Wars, but granite was just too expensive for major construction work, and Bosahan – Constantine's last working quarry – closed its gates in 1993.

Shaping the stone

Quarrying would begin with removing the soil and loose rock to expose the granite, which would be examined to find the 'cleaving-way' joints. Quarrymen would drill holes into these, one man turning the 3" drill while two others took turns to strike the drill head in perfect rhythm. The holes were rammed with explosives, and the huge rock blasted away from the quarry face. To break up the block into workable pieces, steel wedges – *gadgers* – would be inserted between steel feathers and hammered into more small drill holes until the rock split. The boulders would be wrapped in chains, and lifted with cranes to the quarryman's bench or *banker*. Stone cutters such as Roy Guy *(below)* would fashion the blocks into the desired shape and size with bush hammers (with up to 10 blades) and chisels.

Maen Quarry workers in 1926. Quarries needed a skilled workforce – toolsmiths, stone cutters, saw men, polishers, labourers and foremen – trades often passed from father to son. It was an industry fraught with danger, with injuries caused by falling rocks and explosions, rock splinters and dust. The noise was, literally, deafening – the continual crack of mallet on drill-heads and chisels, the clank and rumble of traction engines, the shriek of huge granite-cutting circular saws, and the frequent dynamite blasts.

Features: *a field and woodland walk leading past medieval manors to a scenic creek and the historic waterfront at Port Navas.*
Terrain: *bridleway muddy in winter and after rainfall; some road-walking.*
Duration: *1 – 2 hours. Port Navas is best at high tide.*

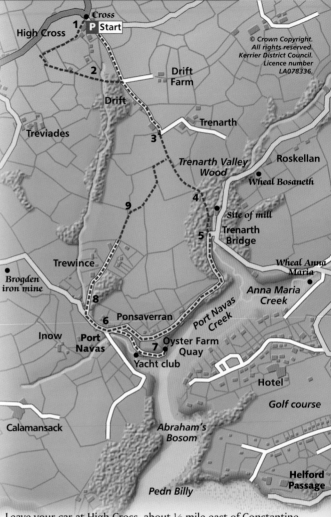

Constantine's crosses

Medieval wayside crosses once marked most of the paths in this book, showing the way to church, or the limits of church lands. You can see some of those that remain – near the parish boundary at Trevease; in the roadside just up from Trewardreva Mill *(page 21)*; and here at High Cross. This one was found in a nearby field and was restored on a new shaft by stonemason Harry 'Dix' Phillips, John Kent of Treviades, Antron Knowles of Mabe and John Olds of Bosahan. A time capsule was buried beneath the base-stone.

Yellow bartsia

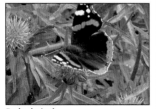

Red admiral

Leave your car at High Cross, about ½ mile east of Constantine. There's space for three or four cars on the grassy triangle behind the old Cornish cross, which was repaired and sited here in April 2000 *(see panel)*, near the restored 18th-century fingerpost.

1 High Cross

With the cross behind you, head south-west across the righthand road and take the footpath through the wooden gate. Follow the hedge on your left and you'll soon pass an opening – this is where the cross-head was found protruding from a hedge. Continue over a stile, head left and you'll eventually reach a splendid granite stile. From the top of the stile you can see, facing west, Brill Hill with its cellphone mast, then the experimental windmill, erected in the late 1980s. Further north are the stone heaps of Retallack Quarry, then the top of Maen Quarry (site of the Tolmen Stone).

Continue over the stile; in late summer you'll be walking through swathes of yellow bartsia and self-heal. If you hear firing, don't be alarmed – the farmers often use bird-scarers to protect newly-planted seedlings. Follow the hedge on your right as you continue up the incline and over the brow, then through a wooden kissing gate in the bottom right corner of the field.

You're now looking over the Trenarth valley, with Budock Vean Hotel golf course in the distance to the right, and to the south, the uplands of the Lizard Peninsula. Down to your right is Trenarth creek, where you're heading.

2 Drift

Continue down the hillside, passing clumps of silverweed and the odd sprig of ragwort and knapweed in summer. Go over the stepping stones, across the stile into the wood, and onto a boardwalk over a stream; across another ancient stile and a small bridge. After 15m bear right, through a plantation of sky-blue mop-top hydrangeas in the private gardens of Drift House.

Head straight across the drive and continue uphill. The path swings left, past a carpet of yellow archangel in early spring, and then through a channel between two wire-mesh fences. Cross the granite stile onto the road and turn right, and continue down the road to eventually reach the drive to Trenarth house.

3 Trenarth

As the road turns left into the grounds of Trenarth, take the track to your right; depending on the season, you might be passing fields of knee-high cabbage or shoulder-high maize. The track continues between high hedges – this is a bridleway so listen out for approaching cavalry.

As the track swings to the right, continue straight on through the opening and into a field; you'll get a fine view of Trenarth house to your left at this point. Follow the hedge under the sycamore, and around the field. As the hedge elbows to the left, carry straight on towards the wood at the foot of the slope. In summer, look out for clumps of black nightshade with its white flowers; a common weed in maize fields, it's not to be confused with deadly nightshade, although its unripe berries are also toxic.

Trenarth

Trenarth, 1950s

Part Elizabethan, part Georgian, Trenarth (Cornish for 'homestead on a high place') has stood here for over 400 years, while the estate dates back to Richard de Trenerth in 1262. The Trenerths married into the Trefusis family of neighbouring Treviades *(page 29)* – a 1658 archway plaque features the arms of both families. In the 18th century the estate passed to the Nicholas family, who added a barn here, a wing there, and later owners added a neo-classical conservatory. This has now been removed, and Trenarth today is a pleasing architectural hotchpotch reflecting the fortunes of its owners over five centuries. The 3-acre gardens and woodland are occasionally open for charity on selected days in summer.

Black nightshade

For a while in the 19th century, Port Navas was at the centre of a small mining district. On the road west to Polwheveral was **Brogden iron mine** which in 1873 produced 2,000 tons of iron ore, and in the valley upstream from Penpoll Mill lay the adits and shaft of **Wheal Bosaneth**, a copper mine worked in the 1830s.

Another mine, **Wheal Anna Maria**, nestled in wooded slopes in the creek just east of Trenarth Bridge. It closed in 1835 after producing just 9 tons of copper in its first two years, but re-opened in 1860 after rich copper and silver deposits were discovered. However, the mine's steam pumping engine couldn't cope with high tide floods of 3,000 gallons a minute, and at one time miners were wading out with water up to their chests. The lure of silver and gold tempted adventurers one last time in 1906, but Anna Maria yet again failed to deliver her booty.

Honey fungus

4 Trenarth Valley Wood

At the foot of the field go through a gate into Trenarth Valley Wood. Follow the steep path beneath sycamores, holly, oak, beech and hazel; in spring the wood is awash with bluebells and primroses. You're on an old cart track – a direct route from Trenarth farm to the valley mill – flanked by moss-covered stone walls, dotted with clumps of deer fern. Through the trees down on your left, where the small engineering factory now stands. is the site of the old Penpoll corn mill – in use up until the 1850s, when John Manuell, 68, was the miller, helped by 14-year-old Joseph Mayn of Lower Calamansack.

5 Trenarth Bridge

After passing through a swathe of montbretia, you arrive at Trenarth Bridge, at the head of Trenarth Creek; the bridge is at least 200 years old (recently strengthened to carry 40-ton trucks). Turn right up the shaded hill along the road to Port Navas, keeping the creek on your left and watching out for traffic. The banks of the lane are dotted with wild strawberries, herb robert, mosses and ferns; and in autumn, crops of honey fungus growing on decaying tree-stumps. At the top of the incline you'll get your first proper view of the river. Beneath you is Trenarth Creek, while the inlet heading up to the left is Anna Maria Creek, named after the silver-lead mine which was once sited on its banks.

Continue along the road, and past the sign for Port Navas. After Oyster House, lean on the gate for a good view of Port Navas Creek; you'll see how the creek opens up into a sheltered circular pool known as Abraham's Bosom. This peaceful creek and the Helford River beyond was home to a secret operations base in World War II, carrying out daring sabotage and rescue raids on the Brittany coast from late 1940 until December 1943. Operating an 'Inshore Patrol Flotilla' of French fishing boats, its team included the Rendle brothers from Port Navas.

The secret agents of the Helford River

If you'd been standing on the shore at Pedn-Billy, at the mouth of Port Navas Creek, on Christmas afternoon 1943, you'd have seen a seaplane tender *(top right)* towing a peculiar-shaped 25ft 'surf boat' *(bottom right)* out to sea. This was the start of a daring mission to rescue shot-down airmen from Ile-Tariec in Brittany. By night a motor gunboat towed the surf boat up the estuary of L' Aber Wrac'h, and the crew, led by cox'n Howard Rendle from Port Navas, rowed silently ashore onto a beach guarded by 3 German gunposts. In two trips they took onboard 32 evacuees, including English and American airmen, and a Sorbonne professor carrying maps of German flying bomb launch sites.

This was the last mission of the secret Helford Special Operations Executive which since 1940 had been making hair-raising night-time crossings to the Breton coast to drop off saboteurs or supplies, and rescue endangered agents and their families. The SOE was based at the houses of Ridifarne and Pedn-Billy, just round the bend from Port Navas Creek, and run by Lieutenant Commander Gerry Holdsworth, and later the Warington Smyth brothers, Bevil and Nigel, whose father Herbert lived at Calamansack. The team included local men Howard Rendle (later awarded the DSC) and his brother Arthur, who maintained the flotilla's engines.

◀ *The Falmouth bus stopping in Port Navas in the 1920s. The reading room and washroom, built by Jonathan Mayn's grandson the Revd James Mayn, is in the centre of the picture. In 2002 it was bought by the residents and transformed into a busy village hall.*

For centuries Port Navas was a quiet creekside hamlet of just a dozen cottages. The villagers worked on nearby farms, had a few tiny fields of their own, and fished in small boats from the creek.

One man was to change all that. Jonathan Mayn was the descendant of a Constantine family which originated (and took their name) from the farms of Maen Pern and Maen Poll *(page 19)*, and later became tuckers and weavers at Polwheveral *(page 15)*. By 1814 the family owned Lower Calamansack, Ponsaverran and much of Port Navas. With the dramatic demand for granite in the early 19th century *(page 23)*, Mayn saw an opportunity and built a substantial quay in 1830 for shipping out local stone, which until then had to be transported by road to Penryn. By 1840 Port Navas was transformed – carts were rumbling along the new quay road to unload granite or pick up coal, or lime from the kiln; schooners were tied up at the quayside; visiting seamen would be eating at Mayn's restroom, attending daily services in the chapel upstairs, or drinking and playing skittles in the new inn, the Jolly Sailor.

Within another 30 years cranes stood high upon the wharf, which now had its own workshop and a nearby smithy. A second quay had been built, and a quay master appointed. The hamlet had expanded, had a washroom and reading room, and in 1894, its own chapel. Villagers worked on the quays, in the nearby mines, at the oyster fishery, and on the schooners. At one time this tiny village boasted six sea captains and five large vessels.

The Jolly Sailor, in its later incarnation as Bates' tea rooms. It closed as a pub in the early 1900s, following a particularly riotous Good Friday night, when a brawl between visiting cockle-pickers, sailors, Wendron miners and locals caused extensive damage.

The decline in granite and the coming of tourism

The boom was short-lived. In the 1900s cheap granite from Norway brought an end to shipments from Port Navas and, except for some coal and fertiliser deliveries, the quays were only used by Falmouth pleasure steamers. Tea rooms sprang up throughout the village, and residents started offering holiday accommodation. After the Great War the Higher Quay became first a coalyard, then a yacht yard and chandlery, and in 1956 a licensed Yacht Club.

Today the village is again a quiet, but thriving, community. The village hall hosts coffee mornings, art exhibitions, talks and workshops, and summer barbecues. The big date in the calendar, as it has been for 80 years, is the Port Navas Regatta, held in August and drawing crowds from afar to watch the rowing and swimming races, the field events, displays by the Falmouth inshore rescue lifeboat, and listen to Constantine Silver Band.

The lure of oysters has made Port Navas a stopping-off point for royalty on many occasions. The Prince of Wales – later Edward VIII – came ashore in the 1930s (pictured), and Prince Charles has been dropping anchor here since 1957.

Port Navas Regatta

Courtesy of Jeff Meadows

The former quay master's cottage

The former garage (left) and the old restroom and chapel

The Higher Quay in the late 19th century, where a cart is loading up with coal from a coastal schooner. The enormous amount of coal shipped in the 19th century was not for use in the home; it drove the steam pumping engines in the tin and copper mines, and powered the granite quarry cranes.

***Lady of Avenel** loading granite 1875*

Sorting and cleaning mussels in the Duchy Oyster Farm.

6 Port Navas

As you reach the bottom of the hill, you'll see Port Navas village hall in front of you. Turn to the left along the quayside; the small ramp at the head of the creek is the only public slipway on the Helford River. Continue along the road towards the yacht club, with the creek on your right; you're walking along a road constructed by Jonathan Mayn of Ponsaverran in 1830 to carry carts to his new quay. You're passing a varied and interesting row of cottages on your left – Creek Cottage was once the quay master's cottage, built in the 1870s; the long building with the wooden balcony and the large doors used to be the village garage complete with petrol pump. The cottage just beyond, with the arched windows, was built in 1832 by Mayn as a resthouse for visiting sailors, with a chapel upstairs (his name appears on a plaque). Some 30 years later a blacksmith's shop was built next door. Old Kiln is the site of Mayn's lime kiln, where imported limestone was burnt to make fertiliser (he used to hold an annual Lime Feast at Lower Calamansack, when the local farmers and builders sat down to a free spread, and settled their lime bills!).

7 Oyster Farm Quay

Mayn's first granite shipping quay is today occupied by the Port Navas Yacht Club. From about 1830, coastal schooners would kedge and warp upstream from Abraham's Bosom to tie up at the quay and unload their cargo of lime, chalk or coal. They would take on board quarried granite blocks, kerbstones and coping, bound for London, Dublin, Cardiff or Dover. In the 1860s two large cranes were installed to lift the granite around the quay and onto waiting ships, and a lower quay was built to accommodate larger vessels. This is now known as Oyster Farm Quay, and to reach it you bear left up past the Yacht Club along the creekside road.

On the quay you'll find four granite blocks, left here when the granite industry – and the port – went into decline in the 1900s. Coal and fertiliser continued to be imported, and seasonal pleasure steamers brought day-trippers from Falmouth. Today, especially in summer, the quay is still the centre of village life, busy with boats, carolares, the August regatta, and children catching crabs. East of the quay is the Duchy Oyster Farm, where four generations of the Hodges family caught, cleaned and sold oysters for over a century.

The Oyster Wars – fishermen versus the Lord of the Manor

The Helford oyster wars raged for centuries. Back in 1659 the Mayn family – tuckers and fullers at Polwheveral Mill *(page 15)*, and the ancestors of Jonathan Mayn who built the Port Navas quays – were taken to court by Sir Richard Vyvyan for illegal oyster-dredging. They lost, but 200 years later the disputes continued: in 1839 three men were given six months' hard labour for stealing oysters, and in 1847 an armed naval cutter from Plymouth was summoned by John Tyacke of Merthen to deal with another outbreak of shellfish pilfering. When the officer refused to intervene, Tyacke took matters into his own hands, blockading the river with boats manned by miners from Breage and Wheal Vyvyan, armed with sticks and bludgeons. Tyacke was paying the Vyvyans the huge sum of £450 a year for the rights to fish the upper Helford, and also had to deliver 100 best oysters *twice a week on Tuesdays and Thursdays at Trelowarren mansion* throughout

Sorting oysters, 1940s

the season. His strong-arm tactics worked: his fishery prospered for the next 60 years, with a depot first at Polwheveral Creek and then, by 1904, at Port Navas, with the Hodges family acting as oyster bailiffs.

Duchy Oyster Farm, late 1940s

In 1910 the Original Helford Oysterage & Fishing Company leased the fishery from the Duchy of Cornwall, and over the last century the farm was run by Macfisheries and then Lindsay Hodges – the fourth generation of the family to do so. Today the Duchy Oyster Farm is leased by Ben Wright, and also processes clams and mussels. Oysters are in season from September to April (months with an 'R' in them) and are not fished when breeding in summer. They're vulnerable to pollution and oyster 'drills' which pierce their shells and suck the soft meat. Once dredged, they are cleaned for at least 42 hours in UV-sterilised water, then shipped to London or the continent.

Retrace your steps along the creek and when you reach the main road turn left past the village hall, built as a washroom and reading room by Revd James Mayn, grandson of Jonathan. Before you leave the village, take a peek at the garden behind the village hall, a peaceful oasis of wild and cultivated flowers – hemp agrimony, gunnera, willowherb, agapanthus and giant hogweed – on the site of Pope's Cottage. As you leave the garden, notice the large slate-hung house opposite – from the 1840s this was the Jolly Sailor, the only pub in Port Navas and owned by the Mayns. If it's open, pop into the charity shop next door, and admire the spick-and-span telephone kiosk. Turn left up the road, and soon you'll pass Pennance House with two figurehead-like statues in a conservatory; a century ago you'd have been tempted to join the day-trippers for one of Graham and Hellencie Roger's cream teas.

Himalayan balsam in Pope's Garden

Treviades

8 Trewince Lane

Turn right along Trewince Lane, passing through the two granite pillars which once marked the entrance of the carriage lane to Trenarth. Continue up the lane, past Trewince House, a former hotel, and the driveway to Bonarth on the right, and head straight between the two granite posts into a hedge-flanked gulley, busy with summer butterflies feeding on knapweed and brambles.

9 View of Treviades

About halfway along, if you take a few steps down to your left, you'll be treated with some lovely views over the former estate of Treviades Manor. Follow the bridleway as it swings left, and continue until you reach the road next to the entrance to Trenarth (Point 3); turn left and retrace your steps up the road, passing the stile you climbed over earlier, past the entrance to Drift Farm on your right, and the hydrangeas of Drift House on your left. Eventually you join the road which leads right to Mawnan Smith; bear left for about 80m to reach your car at High Cross.

From the early 12th century until 1920, the Manor of Treviades had never been bought or sold, but passed down through first the Treviades family and then, by marriage, the Trefusis family. The building too has pedigree, little changed from the 17th century. Hardly surprising, then, that there are tales of ghosts – of a maid who burnt to death, of a phantom rider and sailor. The early records are also tragic; in 1283 Richard de Treviados was on the jury which sentenced Roger de Caryly to hanging, for the accidental death of Richard's young brother Martin.

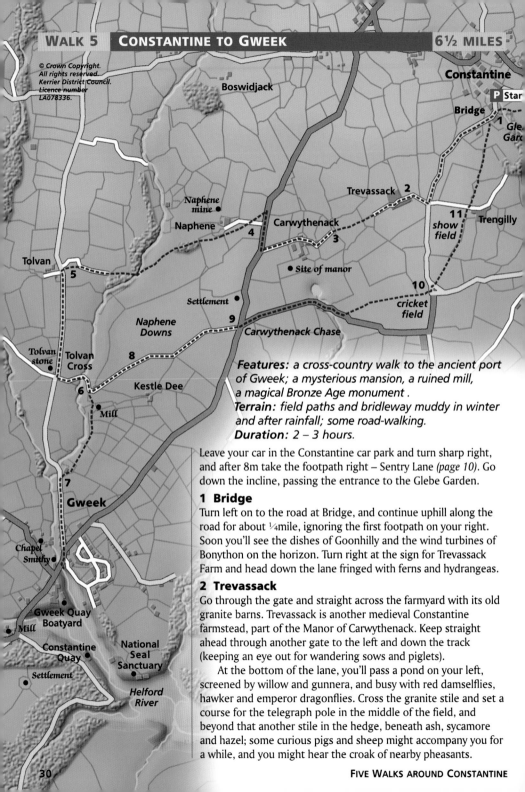

Boswidjack

Constantine

P Star

Bridge

Gle
Gard

Trevassack **2**

11
show
field

Trengilly

Naphene
mine ●

Naphene

Carwythenack

4

3

● Site of manor

Tolvan

5

10

Settlement ●

cricket
field

Naphene
Downs

9

Carwythenack Chase

Tolvan
stone ●

Tolvan
Cross

8

Kestle Dee

6

● Mill

7

Gweek

Chapel
Smithy ●

Gweek Quay
Boatyard

● Mill

Constantine
Quay

National
Seal
Sanctuary

● Settlement

Helford
River

Features: *a cross-country walk to the ancient port of Gweek; a mysterious mansion, a ruined mill, a magical Bronze Age monument .*
Terrain: *field paths and bridleway muddy in winter and after rainfall; some road-walking.*
Duration: *2 – 3 hours.*

Leave your car in the Constantine car park and turn sharp right, and after 8m take the footpath right – Sentry Lane *(page 10)*. Go down the incline, passing the entrance to the Glebe Garden.

1 Bridge

Turn left on to the road at Bridge, and continue uphill along the road for about ¼mile, ignoring the first footpath on your right. Soon you'll see the dishes of Goonhilly and the wind turbines of Bonython on the horizon. Turn right at the sign for Trevassack Farm and head down the lane fringed with ferns and hydrangeas.

2 Trevassack

Go through the gate and straight across the farmyard with its old granite barns. Trevassack is another medieval Constantine farmstead, part of the Manor of Carwythenack. Keep straight ahead through another gate to the left and down the track (keeping an eye out for wandering sows and piglets).

At the bottom of the lane, you'll pass a pond on your left, screened by willow and gunnera, and busy with red damselflies, hawker and emperor dragonflies. Cross the granite stile and set a course for the telegraph pole in the middle of the field, and beyond that another stile in the hedge, beneath ash, sycamore and hazel; some curious pigs and sheep might accompany you for a while, and you might hear the croak of nearby pheasants.

Carwythenack – the mansion that vanished

'A handsome square edifice built with reddish stone and a large cupola on the centre of the roof...' was how C S Gilbert described Carwythenack in 1820. He went on to describe how the house had been 'lately much improved and the plantations, walks and waterfalls considerably enlarged and beautified'. Yet within 60 years maps showed only 'remains of a manor', and today there is little sign that a great house had ever stood here, except a garden wall and two gate-pillars, standing forlornly in a cow pasture.

Carwythenack was once one of the great medieval estates of the area, stretching from Gweek to Brill, with its own chapel, deer park, kennels and dovecot. In the early 14th century it belonged to Sir Richard Stapledon, a judge from the court of Edward I, and later it passed to Edward Chepman of Bosahan, chiefly famous for falling 20 fathoms down a disused mine-shaft when drunk, and being rescued 17 hours later without a scratch. In 1716 the manor was bought by the Hill family of Falmouth, and in 1770 bequeathed by John Hill to Peter Hill (no relation) as a reward for giving him a lift to Helston. In 1820 it was the country seat of William Robinson Hill of the Reform Party, who left it divided between his daughters. The decline was rapid – within decades it had fallen into disrepair, and by 1935 it had been utterly demolished and the stone used to build Lower Carwythenack farmhouse.

3 Carwythenack

Cross the stile and turn left down the concreted path towards Carwythenack farm. You're walking along Kennel Lane, an avenue which in the 18th century led from Carwythenack Manor to the kennels of a pack of hunting hounds. Today it is a shady track passing beneath mighty beech trees; you'll find elder and some recently-planted horse chestnuts too.

At the end of the avenue pass through the farmyard, noticing the granite water troughs and the attractive early 19th century farmhouse with its Gothic arched windows. Continue up the shady track ahead; a field away to your left is a raised plinth of ground on which once stood Carwythenack Manor. If you want a view of the entrance to the former estate, turn left when you emerge onto the main road, and stop at the next gate on your left – at the far side of the field you'll see the fine gateposts and garden walls.

4 Naphene

Turn right at the road, and walk a short distance, passing clumps of late summer hemp agrimony and sneezewort. Continue past the drive to the mid-17th century farmstead of Naphene and climb the stile on your left. Cross the corner of the field and climb the stile in the hedge onto the lane. Cross the stile opposite, follow the hedge on your right until you reach another stile; on the horizon is the RNAS Culdrose control tower. Continue to keep the hedge on your right, passing a clump of teasels. Two centuries ago the fields north of Naphene farm were dotted with shafts, part of the Naphene mine workings. A large adit drained the mine, the water supplying the ponds of Carwythenack Manor.

Cross the stile in the corner of the field and follow the footpath between two hedges, soon becoming a green lane of oak, beech and ivy, bordered with foxgloves, primroses, bluebells, campion and wood sorrel. Through gaps in the trees on your right you'll look down over an attractive wooded valley. After a while you'll descend rough steps formed from rampant tree roots, to reach the stream. Cross over the boardwalk – keeping an eye out for dragonflies and damselflies – and turn left in front of the wooden gate. This section could be muddy after rain.

Hawker dragonfly

Hemp agrimony

Speckled wood butterfly

The Tolvan Stone

For centuries the Tolvan Stone stood beside the ancient ridgeway to Gweek, at the crossroads with the old track from Carwythenack to Helston. It was probably part of a Bronze Age barrow situated in a nearby field, and was regarded with awe and veneration by local people, who thought it possessed healing powers – ailing children were passed nine times through the hole, then laid on the nearby grassy mound with a sixpence beneath their head.

All that was to change when John Moyle built a cottage on the site in 1847. Despite warnings of bad luck, he uprooted the Tolvan, lopped off a few portions to make fence posts, and stuck it behind his cottage as a glorified garden ornament.

The ruins of Mellanoweth mill

Gweek birdlife

Cross a double stile with the stream trickling away on your left, and take the path uphill past a glade, carpeted with bluebells in spring; speckled wood butterflies might join you for this stretch in summer. Cross a wooden stile at the top and go straight ahead, with views to your left down towards Gweek, the roof of the old chapel clearly visible. Continue until you reach a wooden barn, and take the track into the field on your left. Keep the hedge to your right, cross the stile in the corner of the field.

5 Tolvan and Tolvan Cross

Turn left down the main road, passing Tolvan house – this is quite a busy road so listen out for traffic. You're now following the medieval ridgeway to the ancient port of Gweek, the principal route from the mining district of Wendron. Soon you'll reach Tolvan Cross; the house on your right has a King George letterbox in the wall. If you want a peek at the magical Tolvan Stone, turn right at the crossroads and walk a few metres along the track, and peer through the garden hedge to see the large wedge-shaped granite monument standing close to the house.

Return to the crossroads and take the track opposite the house. Follow the lane, passing Watergate cottage on your left before crossing a stream beside an old footbridge. About 50m after the bridge, climb the stile beside a metal gate and into a field; this is the start of a path leading to Gweek (if you prefer to return to Constantine, continue along the lane: Point 8, *page 35*).

6 Detour to Gweek

Head diagonally down the slope towards the trees to reach a wooden gate with a path leading off into the glade behind it. Follow this track, stopping to look at the overgrown ruins of the ancient corn mill of Mellanoweth (Cornish for 'new mill'), the manor mill of the Carwythenack estate in the 17th century and probably earlier; it was still working in Victorian times. The track curves round to the right to reach a granite cattle-rubbing stone; take the steps up into the higher field, turn right, and follow the path between the hedgebanks. Over another low stile, and skirt the bottom of this sloping field and the next. The path curves to the left, and at the top of a slope you'll reach a large granite stile. Continue over this, and along the path, beneath holly and oak trees. The path soon opens out into a field – at the path's edge you'll see betony and burdock amongst the brambles – before passing between two high banks. If you catch a glimpse of something stalking you in the field to your left, don't be alarmed, it's only an ostrich.

7 Gweek

Eventually you'll reach a wooden gate beneath a large elder and emerge onto the road. Turn left and continue along the road, past the Gweek Mission Church, to arrive at the junction opposite the Gweek Inn. Surrounded by mostly 18th and 19th century houses, the centre of Gweek hasn't changed much in the last 100 years or more. You'll find ample opportunities for half-time refreshments at the tea gardens and the inn, or you can pick up a sandwich at the Spar shop and eat it on the bench overlooking the river.

FIVE WALKS AROUND CONSTANTINE

◀ *A top-sail schooner at the lower quay in the late 19th century, with a queue of horse-drawn carts waiting to unload in front of Riverside House. Unable to sail further upstream, large vessels would discharge their cargoes onto rafts.*

Gweek's fortunes have ebbed and flowed for centuries, ever since the Romans were here, shipping locally-streamed tin – the name derives from the Latin *vicus* (village near a fort), and there was a sizeable Roman camp at nearby Grambla Wood and possibly another at Carwythenack *(page 34)*. In medieval times Gweek's importance grew, especially when Loe Bar closed Helston off from the sea in 1302, and it became a thriving Tudor port, shipping out tin and bringing in coal and timber, stone, sand and lime.

Imagine the port during the late 18th century: Norwegian schooners are unloading timber downstream at Constantine quay, or onto waiting barges or rafts; smaller craft – 'lighters' – poled like punts, are bringing smaller cargoes up to the timber and coal yards on the higher quay at the creek head, where the customs house is sited. There's a steady traffic of pack-mules carrying tin ore along the ridgeways from Constantine, Wendron or Helston, to be smelted in Gweek's blowing-house, while carts are laden with corn for the mill, just west uphill from the village.

▲ *The view from the creek-head in 1912 and below, the same view today. Gweek makes an appearance in Charles Kingsley's novel* **Hereward the Wake** *(1866), where the hero's fleet sails 'up a tidal river... between green walls of oak and ash, till they saw at the head of the tide Alef's town'. Hereward trades wine for tin at the port, and later rescues a princess.*

Bound for Philadelphia... or the Arctic!

During the 19th century, the quayside at Gweek was for many destitute families the last time they set foot on Cornish soil; hopeful emigrants would embark here, on vessels such as 'the fast-sailing ship *Caroline*' under the command of John Broad, whose departure was announced in the *West Briton* in 1837: '*copper-fastened, burthen 400 tons, will positively sail, wind and weather permitting, from Gweeke to Philadelphia on Monday the 27th day of March instant, with passengers only...*'

As the century wore on, and the ports of Penryn and Falmouth expanded, Gweek's importance declined. The river became choked with silt, and (except for a secret cargo of tin in 1939 – see page 34) the last major cargoes were shipped out in 1880. Nevertheless, today the riverside is as busy as ever: there's an extensive yacht yard and chandlery on the upper quay, and on the lower quay, a commercial drilling company – Seacore – which sends its skilled staff right around the world, from the Arctic to the Antarctic! The National Seal Sanctuary, on the eastern flank of the creek, is one of Cornwall's most popular attractions.

Courtesy of Seacore

Seacore at the North Pole, during their successful drilling expedition to the Lomonosov Ridge, 2004.

The village in 1904, with the inn to the right of the picture and Alpha cottage just behind it. A century later, the scene is little changed, except for cars, trees and telephone wires – and the Spar Shop!

Spend a while exploring this former port; a short walk along the eastern river bank will give you a panoramic view across the creek to the boatyard, built on the remains of 18th century quay walls. Above the forest of masts you'll see the old quay timber store and office, and to the right, the former quay account house. In the winter the yard is crowded with boats laid up and yachts and motor vessels undergoing refits and restoration work.

If you continue south along the road it curves round to the National Seal Sanctuary, which has been providing a refuge for storm-battered seals since Ken Jones set up base here in 1975. Open daily except Christmas, the Sanctuary includes a hospital, nursery and convalescent pools, an otter enclosure, and is home to a few resident seals which cannot be returned to the wild, as well as some Patagonian sea lions.

Returning to the village centre, just over the handsome 19th century bridge and opposite the entrance to the boatyard, a track to your right leads past some fascinating tumbledown cattle sheds and the remains of the old smithy. Following the main road west from the village brings you to Gweek's huge former corn mill, now converted into apartments, and a thatched lodge house, while Chapel Hill leads past the old Methodist Chapel.

When you're ready, return to the junction opposite the inn, and retrace your steps back along the road, and all the way up the footpath, returning to the lane at Point 5, where you turn right.

The former quay account house

Gweek boatyard, 1987

The old smithy